Poems of August

by Kait Quinn

ALSO BY KAIT QUINN

Clear

I Saw Myself Alive in a Coffin

A Time for Winter

Cover design by Kait Quinn
Cover art by Ken White

ISBN: 978-1-7364839-4-7
Imprint: Kait Quinn Publishing

for the IG *poetry community.*
*we listened to **folklore** together and let it inspire us endlessly,*
our collective words are brewing magic.

CONTENTS

SEVENTEEN

i wish seventeen was filled
with memories better worth remembering,
and i guess there were those weekends
you came home from college, drove me to
empty parking lots, and i swear that i could see the stars
through the roof of your car. but then she'd call,
the blue glow of her catching our sweat like moonlight
illuminates the kind of things that lurk in the dark.

and i guess there was the boy who kissed me quick
on my cousin's driveway and then in the kitchen
and against his truck, how cute he said i was
up on my tip toes, our tongues bubbling
with lemon and lime, and i swear we fell in love
through cell towers and phone lines. but there were a hundred
seventy two miles between us, and i was still hung up
on the boy who didn't want me, so you fell for the nice girl
in homeroom, and i don't blame you.

and i guess there was senior prom,
realizing during the last song that the boy in my arms
might be more than a friend, how he held my hand, kissed me like
everyone was watching, how naturally my palm fell
to his thigh under the table, and the whole night
was a dreamy glimpse of what it would be like—
a daylight kind of love instead of illicit affairs.
but by then the damage to the wiring
between my head and my heart had been done,
and i was leaving for college in three months,
and it was the dream i wanted, not him.

i wish seventeen was filled
with memories better worth remembering,
but if i could go back, would i do anything different?

I SEE YELLOW AND ALL I CAN THINK IS

dear nostalgia, flash me back to sunlight pouring onto limbs locked at knee and elbow. june bugs in the breeze. June romance. cold comfort of known faces and steel-calloused hands. dear nostalgia, drive me to my childhood home, past the farm, next to the playground where C wouldn't hear no, and i swear i'll open the door and run all two miles home in seven-dollar Old Navy flip flops. the flavor of ashes on my tongue. taste of empty. wisdom of the sea. skin made of stars. dear nostalgia, race me to our last day on the lake but bathed in bright blue, tongue sharpened by sunlight, and i will scream *I AM DONE* and mean it—i'll mean it, i mean it, i'm done, i mean it. maybe i can be more sun than moon, my own canary in the dark, sunflower gold and resilient. dear nostalgia, we can try to be friends, but some lines just never seem to bend.

A MARVELOUS TIME

in the next hour,
i'll ruin everything—
paint your flesh blue,
drill my teeth into your bones,
suck the light from your pupils
and the cranberry from your kiss.

the flowers are paper, the wings are wax,
and i'm not civil enough not to light the match.

and you'll question
whether beautiful things still exist,
and i'll tell you:
your skin is an ocean;
your bones strung like pearls,
moon iridescent;
your eyes are gaping mouths, unblinded
and ready to take everything in;
your lips, once bleeding, now blossom
blush peony pink.

this is not an execution—burning the devil
at the stake—this
is a cleansing
that will strip us down to the stardust
and ocean salt we are at the core, who i know we were
before this world turned us
into a war.

it's civility that made monsters of us.
i just want to see what we could be with nothing
but ash and earth to shape us.

BURN

we kissed
and sparks set us glowing,
our limbs live wires—
unpredictable, electric.
we burned like July suns,
blazed like August campfires,
heartstrings tendriling like smoke,
fingerprints branded
to thighs like hot iron.
we were humid dusks,
all firefly bodied,
voltaic heat lightning.
all this time i thought
this was an endless summer
when really,
it was a burning.

WORLD SERIES KIND OF STUFF

picture me
seventeen
high on moon songs
love i didn't have

all i wanted:
ferocious
star-crossed
can't sweat this
folk song
love

WE FELL TOGETHER LIKE AUTUMN,

glowed bright like leaves in October
just before they lose themselves to the frost.
where we once might have had eight feet
of limb between us, we now crunch down
to the same dust. no one would ever
tell us apart come December.

we fell together like cinnamon and clove,
pumpkin and nutmeg—all spice, no sugar;
not even a lick of maple. we steamed into a froth,
then burned each other's throats
on the way down.

we fell together like sweaters drape
around shoulders, believing oversized meant
a perfect fit. you wrapped tight like a crimson scarf
around my neck, and i choked and called it
perfectly splendid.

we fell together like Halloween and graveyards,
promised if death ever came, she'd come for us both.
but one of us was a liar and the other is a cemetery
doomed to spend eternity eidolon haunted.

YOU LIKE THIS POEM BECAUSE
after M. G. Hughes

you like this poem because it's stained
with September nostalgia, crisps
chestnut at the edges, tastes like cinnamon
and coming home.

you like this poem because my heart
pumped it from chest to head to
fingertips, laced it with the salt, stardust,
cigarette smoke of memory.

you like this poem because it arms
its skin but bends in the middle,
feels like putting a face to a dream,
like you were right all along.

you like this poem because your
freckles are all over it, because its aura
burns sapphire and hazel, pupils star crossed,
because you think it is about you.

RUNNING THROUGH YELLOW

stars fall like timeless truths.
i should have known yours—all that steam
and emerald glowing; the way you imposed yourself
on earth, killed everything but the dirt;
a weakness bending my knees,
cracking my ribs like an eggshell;
all that crimson yolk.
but o, my cold hands and all your sun,
candlelight, and galaxy skin. all that
stained-glass moonlight exploding
across my pupils in kaleidoscopic patterns
weaved into wildfires in summer fields.
my feathered heart and pallid limbs
couldn't take the heat—but o,
what a lovely way to burn.

YOU GAVE ME YOUR WORD (BUT THAT DIDN'T MATTER)

after Olivia Rodrigo

promises whispered in motel voices,
summer spent sneaking around,
skipping town. her presence set

the dark on fire. these butterflies,
all along, only paper, ripped
to debris and scattered. your cracked

ego, my broken heart, all the jagged
pieces that would never fit like they did
before i fell in love. i did not open

the way a flower opens. i opened like fish
skinned, gutted, and filleted. if this heart
is a razor, your tongue is a knife, and we are just

a moon song drowning out July's
cacophonous cicada choir, heavy as heat,
thunderous as shit hitting the fan on the ceiling.

summer slips and tangles in the blades,
throats slip beneath the surf, and i'm still ghosted
and awake, writing eulogies for our mistakes.

EVERY POET NEEDS A MUSE (& DARLING, YOU WERE MINE)

elegize me,
hunt the poet.
beloved muse,
make me cry.

i want sad poetry.
want you frozen
in my calamitous grief,

lakes where my heart
once beat.

SLIP

one cough and you miss the canary call.
one blink and you miss a thousand comets.
one bout of blues and summer sneaks past
in an instant.

you slipped away faster.
holding you was like holding water
in my hand.
holding me was like dipping a fist
into molasses and trying to pry it open.

mistakes are made.
dirt gets under our fingernails.
we lose a ring or a bracelet or a pair of eyeglasses
to the lake.
we're only human.

but the difference between mistake
and resolve
is intention.

HONEY HAIKU

hopped in his pickup
hoping for honey. got bees-
wax. jaded so young.

MOTH BELLIED

vintage high
sequin smile drunk
sweat kissing bed sheets
heartbeat disaster
all star and scar
now bleeding

i know
you'll tattoo linger
haunt my what-ifs
smoke strangle me
and i need the thrill
—being porch light keen

come back to me
come back

put on your favorite

KISMET
after Solomon Elijah

i remember you
before my flesh was flesh
and your bone was bone
and we were still one star
yet to explode and split
into trillions of beautifully
misshapen little pieces.

swear i saw you on the other end
of the cosmos. knew the creek bottom
of your eyes before they curved
into their sockets. i knew your skin
would be a map of the constellations.
knew those fingers would be made
for guitar strings. but i never would have guessed
they'd also break me.

there are no words for describing the way i ached
when my heart ripped from yours at earth's birth.
and again, at your own hands.
and ever since, i've been trying to find my way
back to that undischarged star.
it's why i look up at the moon and howl
h o m e.

AUGUST BLACKOUT

salt-rusted memory
twists, guts
like i ever had you.

like i never
canceled plans
in case you'd call.

so much for summer—

august slipped away;
i kept sipping you
like wine

for the hope
of a fall b u r n.

THE SOUND OF THINGS STARTING

sky scraping horizon,
outright dirty lie,
tongue smacked against the roof
of your mouth,
a shattered constellation,
the sound of things starting.

tell me again all the sins
i committed to deserve a heart ruptured
at the seams. i can't even remember
who i was before you,
when my chest was still whole,
bones intact. but i know i miss her more
than i ever loved you.
i know she deserved a first love
better than this—the kind worthy of
movie screens, mixtapes,
hot burst of galaxies at birth.
memories like cicada choirs and sweet tea
instead of pink lemonade
soured in summer heat.

you say that "crazy" women are drawn to you,
like you're just an innocent bystander.
like all the women you've ever loved don't have
one glaring thing in common.
you stepped into this fully armed.
i slinked in with nothing but a heart
ripe for the breaking.

to think, all this time,
it was me i was mourning.

HARVESTING THE LAMB

you've planned this since October.
since the day our love rose
like a corpse from its grave.
you took notes from fall's bleeding. learned
how to make a burning stake,
blood sacrifice look like a blossoming.
you plucked roses from earth, told me i
was just as elegant, just as blushed.
told me we were destined,
i was your favorite,
your little vermillion leaf.
you stroked my heart into singing.
strummed my poems into pearls
i never bothered
to scrape between teeth, testing
for grit or gloss.
you made a lyricist of me.
pulled pulsing stars to film my pupils
with galaxies only i
could see. like you knew
every tease it would take to trick me.

this was not a wooing. this
was a haunting. a gathering
of trust. the kind of falling
where no one plans to catch you;
no longer a question of if but when
your bones will crack against concrete.
it was a slow drain.
a white-laced saunter towards death.

what were you planning on reaping
with these organs, these chunks of my heart,
currant-coated bits of flesh, pearlescent
shards of my birdcage chest?
what harvest did my sparrow lungs provide?
what fruits between my thighs kept
your cheeks plump, sweet incisors satisfied?
what kind of winter were you planning to survive?

LUCIFER

you walked through the door, all those years ago,
sunbeamed and clementine smiled. your boyish grin,
your hand on my back, your tsunami tongue that couldn't
stop flooding my throat with love—where is your halo hibernating
now? what fronts clashed into a storm in your blue skies?
you tornado spun into a stranger, and i am left trampled
on the tail of your tumult. we turn to look in the mirror
and your eyes that once painted me starred and moon
glowing kill me, and you no longer feel like home.
what happened to all those merry endings you promised?
the strands of i-love-you's stringing across our pillows like pearls?
what sun melted your wings?
where is your halo hiding?

ALL THE GOLD

when the world—swallowed in grey snow,
glistening gold in the firelight of apocalypse
—was ending, i met you. i was a bloodied blanket
of a body, you the promised salve for every wound.
how you slinked in like fog, blinded like diamonds,
bled blue like you were born from the same world
as rainwater. your silence cuts me softer now but fillets me all the same.
i should have intuited what the moon was trying to tell me
when dark clouds wrapped their palms across her full,
glowing mouth. no one likes a mad woman. a command-the-tides woman.
a drag-the-howl-from-the-wolf's-mouth woman. you were not
a savior but a hunter trying to ensnare me with futures and flattery.
not all the gold, guns, girls in the world could be enough
to feed your appetite. what a fool to think i was. what a self-
violation: constantly running back into your arms. and if you kissed
me now, i fear i would not have the strength to rip that seam again.
you're permanent like a bad tattoo, and how i wish the apocalyptic
void had swallowed me, too, if only to have never been imprinted
with the memory of you.

WHEN YOU HAD NOT TOUCHED ME YET
after Lord Huron

and my pores had not yet drowned
in cheap cologne, eyes starless, ribs
uncracked, heart still heart shaped,
now smeared and splattered across
the insides of my chest. i cannot stop
committing arson. cannot assume
grace's bones, unsuffer this blue. cannot leave
these embers to ash dwindle. i shake them,
just before they've finally burnt out.
i call these ghosts from their cemetery slumber
out of spite. i clink glasses and feign fires
rekindling, relish the day i get to watch
the hope in *your* eyes drain. we are
undying. i make sure of it. if i am to be scarred,
so are you. may i find peace and may you
never rest nor go gently
into the fitful night.

WITHOUT CEREMONY

without goodbye,
without answers,
without any acknowledgment that love
once flowed sap sweet between us.

you are the war i carry.
the ellipsis, the echo,
the unfinished business
that's made me more ghost
than woman. and if it weren't
for this gnawing in my heart,
this iceberg in my chest,
bones splintered, fingers bloody
from picking through all
those barbed wire lies and sanguine promises
fallen from grace,
i'd think i wasn't really here at all.

truth:
did you ever love me?
do i keep you up at night?
did you fuck her before you decided
to call us quits?
was she worth it?

dare you to tell me.
dare you to call me crazy.
dare you to drive me mad.
dare you to scream to the moon about it
like she's prone to bend ear to men.

carry me to her edge,
and i'll show you what the night makes me.
how she whips my August breeze
tornadic, tugs my still waters
to hurricanes, pulls claws
from these nectarine fingers,
kindles fire in my snowfall throat.

i'll show you that this baby bird heart

can scorpion sting just as well
as she can sugar sing.
i'll show you the living
are capable of haunting.
my goodbyes are never
without ceremony.

MAD

sting strike
kill sing

fuck boys breed
mad woman,
breed witch

dirty work—
hydra, claws,
finding mad

taking my time
watching you writhe,
mastering—

a good witch knows
—mad

TOXIC TRUTH

i pop into your head at night
porcelain limbed, pretty in pink,
betty wronged, and mary pure.
i was your good girl. complicit.
i was your madonna. innocent.
hurting me was the worst thing
you ever did.
but what if i told you
that i spent my twenty-first birthday
making out with another man?
so star dazed, our friends had to unwrench
our grasping hands so we could go
our separate ways—him to hope, me to you.
what if i told you we went on a date
a few weeks later? that he kept coming back
to my doorway because i wouldn't kiss him
goodnight. what if i told you i wish i had?
what if i told you i didn't feel bad
because where the fuck were you?
which of your other girls were you in that night?
what if i told you i splayed my thighs
across the lap of a future preacher,
just minutes
before you picked me up and took me to bed?
that i knelt down in worship over his cock.
mouth blossoming against mouth,
our crotches pressed hot together.
what if i told you i stood up, ran to the next room,
cried, then called you?
what if i told you i wish i hadn't
because who were you sneaking off with then
for months behind my back?
what if i told you i fucked someone else just hours
before we made *us* official?
that my hair was still wet from his shower.
that it was his scent clinging to my neck.
that it was his tongue you were tasting,
not mine. what if i told you i kept
my own secrets for three years?
would that make me bad too?

would that make us twin stars
in twisted pas de deux?
would that convict me and absolve you?
would that shed a muddy tint
on my fine peach glow? drain the rose
from your swollen pupils? fuck it.
let this ripe flesh rot.
let this flame fade to ash.
let this flower lose its shape, its nectar,
every unblemished petal.
either we were perfect for one another
or all wrong, wrong, wrong.
you want the toxic truth?—darling,
we were doomed from the start.
executioner, set the guillotine for two.

THE WAKE

weeping sun
ashes our grave

i haunt you
in ghostly grace

you curse my heart,
my blood, my bones

at the wake
had to toss blame

stain the good years—look
at me ricochet

THE PERILS OF AUGUST

slow drain. shimmering edges. clash of things ending against things beginning and not knowing up or down or forward or back. that at any moment, "crystal baller" could jump out of the stereo and take me back to the summer that set my greatest downfall burning.

and when you were a kid, the only perils of August were whether or not your parents had money for new school clothes or if it was gonna be hand-me-downs, eighth grade looming on the horizon, letting the fireflies free, taking the thumbprint frogs back to the creek and wondering if our spoons were deep enough to scoop down enough stars to fill the now-empty coffee tins.

otherwise—we   were   f r e e.

when you are young, nostalgia hasn't been born yet, doesn't creep up on you like ghosts. only Octobers were haunted. now, i see him everywhere. and i desperately miss those long summer days when my only worries were mosquitoes and sunburns. now a fear looms beneath everything: skin cancer. sweat stains. sand in every crevice. mascara running. heatstroke. that he and i are just another summer fling.

when i was seven, i was a peach sweetening in the August sun. now my eyes are swollen sapphires and my pupils drip ink and blue stains my cheeks and every season feels like winter.

every season freezes over, if i let it.

IF YOU'D BEEN THE ONE

i say yes
instead of no.

i   stop   running
and f a l l,

bleed pennies,
pool my wishes
into you.

i dream adventure,
paint smeared on the sheets,
nesting, and rosé f l o w-
i n g
sweet to the grave.

would've been fun if—

NOCTUARY

i'm listening to "my tears ricochet,"
and i'm dancing under the pale moonlight
with my favorite ghost. and we are water sloshing
over the precipice. we are capsized.
but we keep coming back with moon's tides.
can't stay away. can't stop carving your name
into my bones. didn't have it in me
to rest in peace.
to bury all the pieces.
pierce through
to the other side of darkness.
my favorite season is the one
that's always dying.
my favorite mood
is playground blues.
my favorite blanket is nostalgia.
my favorite ghost is you.
dance with me
over the broken glass
till our heels are red birds,
our souls plasmic stains—
bruisey and vermillion
—smeared like immortals
across ink black oblivion.

LOVE IS NOT A BROTHERS GRIMM FAIRY TALE

September dreaming
of saffron-skied nights, back when we had nothing
but each other and our skin dipped
in twilight, and from just
the right angle, to some far off pupil,
we   are   stars—
gods in the heavens inventing tragic.
i am so blinded by the silvered slivers
burning from our seams, i throw back
this emotional cocktail of hate
candy coated in adoration.

you were always marking me in bloodstains
i mistook for hunger and, fuck, i felt like a queen
draped in moonlight and crimson
and the dark gaze of your desire.
they say there's a freedom in the fall—
and, darling, did i feel weightless—but
they don't tell you what happens
when you hit the ground.
how the lungs rupture
and the bones break and the heart pulls
itself in half when it aches.
i'll never erase these stubborn scars.
i'll never deep breathe this pulse to a rest.

do lips bruise? do teeth poison?
do we call lovers "flames" because they burn?
is it still called love if it hurts?

"HOAX" ON REPEAT

smoking wounds
scream violet
bleed crimson
burn blue

bless skin
still barren
bless stomachs only
butterfly beaten
bless the broken hearted's attempts
at rose gold lacquering

these veins fester
these heartstrings pull
these joints hang crooked

you left
scars so bone
rooted
i am all sea
bruise
and sadness

grave desecrated
thread snagged
and unstitched

we are
each other's unweaving

LOVE LIKE LAKES

vintage jacket, brand new heartache.
we forget that we are fragile. that when a lake
freezes over, too much weight, one wrong step
can crack her open. that her only response
is to swallow. between the two of us, too much storm.
we weren't making it out of those depths alive,
but we kept jumping in anyway. i keep jumping in.
i keep waking the dead just to feel ache, just to feel
something. i always preferred the knife of a snowstorm
to the sun's July honey drizzle. sometimes i think
you only wanted me when i was peach ripe. sometimes
i think i was the frozen lake that kept swallowing
you up and spitting you back out. but you kept coming back.
you keep coming back. we only know how to drown
in a love like that.

YOU SAID FOREVER NOW I DRIVE ALONE PAST YOUR STREET

after Natalia Vela after Olivia Rodrigo

the one with the same name as the ex who left you
galaxied and shattered. and i wonder if you still keep my book on
your shelf, if you bought the new one, how many tongue
your coffee table, spine your walls, what you'll tell her
about the girl who wrote the poems you collect on the mantelpiece.
i am the backbone to everything: ball and socket to every
step, silhouette to every dream, the golden carrot you can never
quite reach—still you stay so damn hopeful, it's almost
charming—pot of gold, sunrise on horizon,
oil that keeps your love burning, me scarring, trail
of lights that guide you home. expect a crash landing.
expect to come undone. expect these poems
to pull every thread, unstitch every seam.
call the priest, buy the sage, expect ghosts
and upturned graves. i can't stop breaking us apart,
disecting every vein and organ, putting the pieces back
together in alphabet tapestries i can't stop unraveling, then weaving
into another what if. what if we were older? what if i never
gave you my number? said yes to the boy who kissed me
on the driveway in Texas with his chapsticked lips
and Sprite-soaked mouth? what if i new better? what if i'd ever
learned to drive? coughed the feathers from my throat
and let those sirens sing? what if we said forever?
what if this time we meant it?

MEMORY LANE

my memory lane is a real place
where we knock our moth wings against porch lights.
we had a way of mistaking anything bright
for the stars, each other for celestials.

my memory lane is cobwebbed corners
and unswept floors because i'm not ready
to sweep away our dust, fingers retracing
eulogies of us: *here lies*
the greatest love story never told.

i want to be forgotten and reminded,
hated and admired. i am endlessly
besotted. high on moon beams. drunk on
the scars on my heart where you ripped
it at the seams—they still sting, still bleed.

my memory lane is October nostalgic,
and i want to curl up in it like earth is your chest,
trees are your arms, wind is your breath
warming my algid skin till i am all steam
and condensation. all this gold is ruthless.

my memory lane is second chances woven
into heartstrings. and thirds and fourths,
and i am reminded why we ricocheted off
each other's bones, nailed the coffin,
buried this love in a six-foot grave.

taylor said it best when she sang
those gutting lyrics—how the best films
aren't made and the greatest loves are dead.
here lies the impressioned heart
where you used to rest your spinning head.

IN WHICH I RETRACE MY STEPS INTO CIRCLES

September when I first met you,
but the leaves had yet to amber.
That summer was so triple-digit thick,
I never would have guessed there'd ever
be a fall so kaleidoscope explosive.

Right before I dream, I conjure you,
memories like old toys for heartstrings.

I will never feel the fit of your hand in mine
again. Will never know every constellation
of your skin. I will never feel the burn
of looking into your pupils, like staring
down the sun. Will never feel if our lips
still know their chemistry. Already
I've forgotten the way you taste.

I learned to hate you to forget, but hatred
is still an attachment—now you are an itch
I want to scratch, slap, pull deep inside me
until I can't feel you anymore.

I don't want to feel you anymore.
I don't want to look up at skies of gold
and crimson and think of that first October
before the apples turned to rot.

I don't want to keep dreaming
questions that take me to your door.
When I get there, I never know
how or why or what to say.

I've run out of steps to retrace—
you are not the home I'm looking for.

THIS IS NOT HOW IT WENT BUT HOW IT SHOULD HAVE WENT

i take the bullet, accept the puncture to heart and bleed out.
i let the space where steel made a home in me widen when i pluck
the thing out. i let it gape. i let whatever wind sweeps through its
canyon wail into the night. i stain my cheeks in salt; i do not let
him wipe my tears, carry them close in his pocket.
i do not let him have his cake and eat it too. i take all the damn cake
for myself and leave him none. i leave him. i do not let him
tie strings around my fingers, implant magnets into my bones that pull
only toward him. i face my north pole toward his. i back away. i don't
waste three more years being made a fool. i make friends with the girl
he fucked behind my back. we write poems about him—scathing ones
—and publish them in DIY books we litter across campus. he finds one.
we laugh about it. i grieve for *her* when she dies—instantly in a car crash—
not just for what she represents. i date every guy i ever doubletaked over
americanos in Meadows. i date the manager of the Mexican restaurant
where my best friend works—the one with the blue eyes, soft tongue.
i kiss the tall stranger who picks me up off the sidewalk on 4th
just to see what it would feel like to hold something that small.
i don't just wonder what it would feel like to kiss a man over six feet
tall. i just do it. i never look back. my heart fills and closes
the bullet wound. it never festers, only seals
that door closed. i never open it again.

I NEED YOU CLOSER,

he said. but i am about as
attainable as horizon—no,
as ocean rushing toward
you only to slink away. i know this,
somehow, is worse.

you want to drink me in,
but you gag and choke—my
brine not made for your throat.
i don't think anyone could
swallow me, feel me wash over

their skin and settle.
if i was going to call any shore
home, it would have been yours.
but somehow your whale lungs were still
not quite large enough to withstand me.

LET ME SHOW YOU WHAT WOULD HAVE NEVER BEEN

beneath a moon waning
toward the darkest night of the year,
we rise from the buried bones
of our decayed love
in the heart of a lonely winter. we are
undead creatures wrapped in new skin,
as if your heart is not still three sizes too big
and mine is not still broken.

i come to you in temporary revival
to show you how multi-faceted and whole
i've become, every side of you
that ever hurt me, then made me dizzy
till the stars gathered in my pupils and left you
g l i s t e n i n g.
that love business is powerful,
and lust can crack you at the knees.
but let me show you what we never would have been
so that we can rest these ghosts in peace:

we never would have swept up all the pieces—
soles of our feet teething with glass—and we'd get so tired
bleaching all that blood out of the carpet.
we never would have built a home with wood floors
of trust and sage walls of laughter—our foundation being
irreparably cracked.
your sweet tooth would have swelled
into glutton. i'd have soured past the point
of return. you never would have gained the courage
to crack spine open and lay heart bare.
i'd have never blossomed.

these keys are shiny, but they don't fit,
and if we played out all these what-ifs,
we'd shatter all the memories that are good,
and there's already enough bad blood between us.
so back, back, back to the grave.
some futures are better left unexplored.

BROKEN NIGHTINGALES

summertime bleeds on the horizon.
silhouettes of nightingales meet and break
like distant kisses at dusk.
the pink underneath like our skin,
sticky in the August sun.
i am ready to shed this weathered
flesh, these freckles,
you. we were something: tangled roots,
water spilling into dirt,
ripe peaches on the tongue,
an effortless blend of chords you knew
just how to pluck to make me sing.
how to make me curl up tight, jaw locked,
saliva collecting like glue between my teeth.
we're down to the pit.
hear the silence. hear how fast this heart races,
how it slows, how it snaps, how it howls in the night
searching for a home. i don't belong here with you.
but i wanted to.
i swear i wanted to.

I'M LISTENING TO TAYLOR SWIFT'S NEW ALBUM
after Natalia Vela

for *Brittany*

and i'm thinking of frogs and creeks and old lovers
but mostly of fifteen because i've got "seven" on repeat.
and i'm thinking about how you cut your bangs too short
and how it wasn't that bad, even though it took a whole year
to grow them back. i'm thinking about weekends at your aunt
and uncle's house, *lord of the rings* marathons, weed in the cookies,
how my dad didn't notice your irises swimming
in pools of milky pink. and i'm thinking about the night
we cried in the movie theater,
when rosalee gives pete her version of his six smiles speech.
and then again during the *Friends* finale.
and one last time on the curb outside your aunt and uncle's house the day
you moved back home to Louisiana. no one understood my saltwater soul
like you did. and i'm thinking about that time we bought
a bag of kolaches and walked at least a mile to give them to Yates
who probably didn't give a fuck but called us sweet anyway.
i'm thinking about the first christmas after you left,
the four-hour drive from Houston to Baton Rouge, squished among
your cousins in the back seat because that was how much it was worth—
seeing you again. and i'm thinking about how you told me your dad
would probably tackle me and he did and i thought it was weird
but i didn't say anything. i'm thinking about how i had to tell you
about my first kiss over the phone instead of on the four-post bed
in your West U. bedroom. i'm thinking about the weekend i blew you off,
when you came to visit from college, for the boy who treated me like shit.
how you told me straight up, "he's a dick," because you were the only
person i'd ever known to tell me like it is. and i still refused to see it.
i'm thinking about how during your next visit, i dropped everything.
how you were a mama and i'd been making better choices in men
and we were all grown up and reminiscing
and remember that time you cut your bangs too short?
and i'm thinking about the year i sent you letters and where you were
when i sent them and how when your best friend shared the address
on your facebook page, i immediately grabbed an envelope and a stamp
because of course i was going to write to you. of course i was. no question.
and i'm thinking about how easily you can lose touch
with the kind of best friends you swore were forever,

down to the first apartment plans and maid of honor dresses.
and i'm thinking it's been awhile. i should check in.
i'm thinking that despite the distance and the silence
and the ghost feeling of it all,
i've still got big love for you, babe.
the kind that sticks to your ribs like a folk song.

FUCKING IN MEMORIAL PARK
after Ella Frears

i'll meet you where the roots tangle
like young lovers beneath the soil.

o, if the trees sheltering
the deepest parts of Memorial Park
could speak, they would heave
sighs we left in the sap-sticky cracks
of their bark.

from then on, every time a boy
slipped a hand beneath my blouse,
up my blue jean skirt, i'd swear my knees
were caked in dirt.

i'm still pulling twigs and 2004's
dead leaves from my hair.
still feel you breathing soft
against my neck when i press
earth to ear.

a burning maple like that
could leave a girl weak in the ankles.
kick my feet out from under me
like you did then. make me feel
wanted and fifteen blossomed
—spread of hot petals—all over again.

you're the one past that doesn't come back
to haunt me. but i wish you would, so i wander drunkenly
through every forest i can grip my soles to,
taking their mud stains with me,
leaving the last woods' dead June behind.

lover, meet me where
roots tangle. paint me earth
bruised at the shins.

WASN'T I BEAUTIFUL?

"Wasn't I beautiful?
Wasn't I fragrant and young?

Look at me now."

       — from "Medusa" by Carol Ann Duffy

dead flora withered. nectar drained.
March snow pallid. your discarded muse,
i have no songs left for you in these caved in
sacs of lungs. ocean depths ice cracked over,
skin once ripe as a peach in late July now shriveled,
sagging with rot. i am a mirrorball shattered
into a million pieces; nothing i could give you
is whole. there are no cosmos to discover
behind these pupils. only lush shadows that lift
to vast plains of grief. i am the wasteland, the unvoiced
forgotten. split me open to the silence of cicada
skins clinging hollow to porch swings and bark.
i am not the slow-dripping honeycomb nor the siren
wail of tragedy. not sun cresting nor moon waxing.
but for the briefest moment, wasn't i beautiful?
eyes bright with garnet? hair September creek
water glistening? throat canary exquisite?
tongue the perfect shade of rouged peony pink?

TO THE BOY WHO THINKS ALL MY POEMS ARE ABOUT HIM

danger, darling.
keep your heart out of this.
paint dreamscapes on
your own fences.
understand: i sing this fire,
cascade ocean blues
for   me.

you will never find peace.

IN WHICH I LISTEN TO *FOLKLORE* AND DREAM OF WAKING UP IN 2006

stretching my arms into a lover's cardigan
instead of squeezing into scuffed heels and
pinning up a cheap black corset, like i knew what i was doing.
but i wasn't the kind of girl boys liked
to drape their oversized sweaters around.
no one wanted to linger in my scent. every four a.m. stack
of pancakes, glass of orange juice, gifted cigarette was not an act
of endearment but a hoax—i'm no betty; i was bred
for illicit affairs. i belonged to no one and everyone and worshipped
the ground lana spilled her inky guts on like she was the last
great american dynasty. just to feel like i chose this.
but i'm not mad. these tears ricochet off concrete
into stars, dip their fiery tails
into sky's ink, and f a l l
back to earth, to the lakes as poetry.
i can craft alphabet into art out of anything—this is me trying
to pull invisible strings like silver linings out of everything
that ever hurt me. like the way he didn't listen when i said no.
like the way he didn't even check my pulse.
like the way you dirty finger fucked my heart
without even bothering to wash her off first.
like the way i tasted her on your tongue. like the way you ran off
with her into the sunset and left me for dead
in desert exile. no explanation, no goodbye,
not even a damn glass of water, and
you   were   not   the   one.
seven years to epiphany.
three more to peace.
and now i'm mirrorball faceted and August glowing.
look   at   me   s h i n e.
but i keep a bit of the mad woman you made me.
for the blood.
for the teeth.
for the poetry.

JAR OF DIRT

i make a meal of every plum tree,
a home of every sunset,
a salve of honey, baptismal font
of sea, a poem
of every constellation,
gut instinct of every twig
snap and shuffle of leaves,
a healing bath of
all   that   moonlight.

i've got a jar of dirt to remember
where i came from and where i go
when i set myself burning.

and from the earth i'll grow—
depth and breadth and height
and skin that reaches for the sun,
knees that swing from the crescent,
amber in my scars,
pupils wide enough to swallow
all   those   stars.

and every birthing season, i hope
i come back without any memory
of us.
and i hope i don't.

i've gotten so attached
to this shade of blue—
this saltwater teal,
this January dusk.

SHOULD HAVE SAID YES

i knew i had a crush on you
when your friends took up the booth and left us—
table for two, Taco Bell in Cedark Park.
we both hated the food but ate it anyway.
what else was there to do?

every crush that ever pulsed through me
was instantaneous. at first sight.
you were no different and you
were nothing like the rest and i think too much
about how i should have said *yes*,
but i was so damn stubborn.
so good at grasping the fleeting instead
of the tangible.

you visited me in my dreams last night,
married with a kid, just like you are now. in real life.
i slept in your bed and pissed off your wife,
but by the time i woke up, i had apologized
for trying to kiss you, and she and i had morphed
into best friends, day drinking at a music festival,
inches away from stevie nicks. and i let you go.
not even my subconscious will let me have you.

when you dream about someone,
do you sneak into their dreams too?
is your dream the same as mine?
did we meet in some other realm,
or did i just imagine it?

i woke up this morning with "first day of my life"
on repeat in my head, and i wonder
if you hear that song and think of me?
if i called you "starshine"
would it still hit you behind the knees?

if there is such a thing as the one
who got away, you'd be mine.
think you would have been
my personal best.

THE NEW FOLKLORE

summer spent counting tiles,
counting all the plums we couldn't reach
at the top of the plum tree,
grinding bones into every cushion,
losing blood, sticking to the mattress. i forgot
what grass feels like against skin,
what a rush of vitamin d does
to a dragging brain and draining cheeks,
how evergreens smell, how brine tastes,
how long it takes sand
to dry and crack off your wet toes,
how bright the moon glows
when she's good and full and unapologetic.

is it easier to stay afloat in the ocean than a lake?
i wouldn't know. haven't jumped in since i was seven-
teen and seal slippery, nursing a sunburned foot
with a pint of ben & jerry's. but i know
that treading water in a lake feels like trying to do—
pay the bills, write two books, make dinner before
the produce goes and save the animals
and don't forget about breonna
and elijah, donation here, donation there and where's
your mail-in ballot and wash your hands, wash your mask,
wash your fruit, remember to play with the cat,
don't think of him, don't think of him, don't think of him,
text your best friend instead, it could be worse—too much at once.

and sometimes i just want to f l o a t.

and listening to *folklore* for the first time
was like inhaling wet, salt air in a desert.
like riding the foam to shore.
like blink and you'll find yourself barefoot
on the coast. like unstitching wounds
and digging out ghosts.
August crashed over me like a wave,
and i couldn't tell which way was up
or down or if it even mattered.
i just took a breath

and let it take me.

i want to go where newborn sea turtles go
when they chase the moonlight home.
but this isn't our season.
summer's the new folkore.

GROWING PAINS

my pupils crack under the light
of the film reel, salt and the flashbacks
staining cheeks. i remember bleeding
in all the buried places you wounded me—
who would believe?
my heart snapped at so many sinews,
i still feel it slap against my lungs,
stick to my ribcage when i'm flat on my back,
paralyzed. i remember everything i wish i'd forgotten
most. i barely remember who i was
before men. only that i was simultaneously so sad
and so sure, and i can't explain that dichotomy.
i've been swimming in the blues since i was five
and billy ray cyrus was the only person
who could put this ache and break into words
i understood. i don't know what other ocean to dive in.
my head splits piecing together every wrong turn,
every epiphany, every glaring flaw traced back
to what played out before me as a child.
i remember the grind of bone against bone
from being held too tight; the knot of wings folding
in on themselves instead of breaking skin, spreading,
and catching the wind. i remember being an open book
everyone kept trying to close, a storm to be quelled,
my waves crashing against stone shores.
and now my cervix gets scraped out
a little more each year because all of the things
we   don't   talk   about. i just wanted to be told that i was worthy,
that i could be a knight instead of a princess,
that i could use my tongue like a sword,
these limbs as a shield. that i could do anything
as long as i was happy and safe. i wish someone had told me
about my inheritance, all these blues in my blood and how
not to drown in them.

THE POET AT SEVEN
after Erika Sánchez after Larry Levi

feet in the creek,
frogs in our palms,
homemade paint—in berry reds
and clay orange and nothing but our fingertips
to paint with—for the teepee grandpa built us,
butterhorn stuffed and gooey handed,
charred marshmallows tugging off our sticks
in glistening strings of moonlight
and sticking to our bellies,
and other beautiful things.

and i think that forest is haunted.
think the dogs meant
to steal my blue clogs when it was muddy out.
and sometimes i'd swear i'd see coyotes
lurking between the brambles. sometimes i think alfie
was part wolf, part guardian angel.
and sometimes, after he died,
i'd go too far into the woods,
searching for his pearly ghost—
think that's why i'm not afraid of wolves.
sometimes i'd swing too high—
think that's how i got this fear of peaks.

i wish i'd spent more time in the weeds.
wish i'd chased the dogs back.
wish i'd howled into the night and been brave enough
to wait, listen for the coyote to yelp back.
wish i'd played pirates instead of cowboys and indians.
wish i'd gotten the truth instead of America's
erasured history lesson.
wish i'd known you when i was seven,
when dirt under our fingernails had
an entirely different meaning.
wish i'd sat in the bluebonnets just
a little longer, damned the rules and plucked Texas
out at the gnarled roots.
wish i'd pressed her into a book,
kept her blue forever.

JUNE BUGS

back in Austin, back in the sweltering
and the air your arms had to push through
like an ocean, the june bugs would crawl
under the inch-wide crack beneath my door.
i'd find them, almost always, as little corpses,
anywhere within three feet of the tiled foyer.
as if the ac-blasted atmosphere, crisp and clear
as a creek, was to those little bronze beetles
like a vacuum to a lung. as if crawling out
of all that swamp air was like a fish
washing up on a waterless shore.
and sometimes i'd find one wobbling among the dead,
lone survivor of the apocalypse gasping
for murky breath, and i'd play god—quicken death
with a crunch. or sometimes i'd find one
slamming its sugar-shelled body against the walls,
as if to fling itself out of its misery. or as if
just trying to find a way back out
into the humidity. i think about that a lot—why i didn't
just sweep the ones still living out the front door.
how easy it would have been to pluck one up
between my fingers and place it gently in the grass,
just four feet from the threshold. but i hadn't yet learned
to love everything. hadn't yet discovered a salve for pain.
had only ever learned to kill what bleeds. to hate a thing
for its faulty reputation, instead of getting down on the ground,
flat on my stomach, to examine that golden underbelly,
the leather-like sheen of its hard-shelled back, the gossamared
wings lying in wait beneath. i wonder if they'd come in
from the east, all emerald and metallic, if i'd have bothered
to show some compassion, or if they'd be just as much
a nuisance to my dingy carpet. and i'm thinking about
everything i miss in Texas: rolling hills, h-e-b, kolaches
and blue bell before i went vegan, fields of bluebonnets
sprawling like a violet sea, montrose, tacos at bouldin,
the sorin oak, my best friend, all the roads
you drove with your hand gripping the back of my neck.
and i'm thinking about all the things i don't miss:
the triple digit heat, the politics, the playground parking lot
where i said no and he convinced me otherwise,

the cockroaches, the road rage, skin sticky
with sweat, ghosts, you
stepping on my heart with a crunch.
never thought i'd miss the june bugs, knocked on their backs,
legs flailing uselessly toward the sun.

WHAT LINGERS

one does not plan, after death,
to go about haunting.
but here we are, ghostly ships aiming
for each other in the night,
restless as spirits
still clinging to a realm they cannot grasp.

i'll never tell you how much i bled out
for you. how many times my teeth sunk
into your flesh without you ever knowing it.
i'll never tell you whether or not you linger
like a ghost ruling the typewriter in my brain.
i will tell you my chest is fine.
this poem is not about you.

what do the dead want
other than to burn
in scarlet flame—*please
notice me*—cover up
in gold leaf, and rest?

there is no good way to break a heart.
there is only a wish to fill the cracks
with moon dust—shimmering silver
—and find peace.

WHEN DAISY TOLD GATSBY SHE WISHED SHE'D DONE EVERYTHING ON EARTH WITH HIM
after Chelsie Diane

but i didn't want to do everything on earth with him. i only wanted
to set the stars in motion, command blood and marrow like moon
moves ocean. i wanted every kiss to bruise into galaxies. i wanted to come
with skin supple and peached and leave with scars like constellations.
i wanted to name them eros and aphrodite. i wanted two skins
melting like candle wax, then melding into one. i didn't want to know
which limb was his, whose hand held whose, what ankle was mine.
i wanted smashed dishes and pillows on fire. i wanted every touch
to send me shattering. i wanted my breath to crawl out of my throat on all
fours, all animal clawed, spine nailed to wall. i wanted a love that burned
cerulean, crimson as October, and i didn't even care if it died in the end.
i wanted a star-crossed love that stuck to my ribs like honey, pelvic bones
like caramel, rich and worthy enough for a lifetime's worth of poetry.

WE ARE THE THINGS WITH FEATHERS

i took a midnight journey to hope
beneath a canvas dusted with stars
ripe and plump for the wishes
salivating on my tongue.
but like the horizon, hope is an ever present thing
incapable of ever being reached.
still, i keep my sights on her with my doe eyes
to keep the nausea of living with salt waves in my belly
at bay.
                                     there is something divine about the space
where the sky and the ocean meet,
like dusk could be lifted like a veil, reveal
a spiritual realm underneath, a world
where we are the ones with feathers
and hope is a nectar that falls from the sky
right into our open gullets, filling our stomachs
until we ache with it.
they say youth know nothing
about hope, but what makes you think
there is not a beating heart to this make believe?

WHAT ABOUT THE LAST TIME YOU FELL IN LOVE

what about tofu chorizo tacos and splitting
the oatmeal cookie sandwich? what about dreaming
of licking the icing center off your lips?
what about yo-yo ma in your ears and marie
antoinette in my pupils? what about buzz?
what about my arms around your waist and the wind
around my arms? what about a single train of thought that turned
into a full-page poem, header to footer, margin to margin?
what about jose's "heartbeats" cover and my back pressed
against the bathroom mirror, thighs splayed across
the counter? what about, after five months, coming home?

what about the first time? what about third eye blind
and sex on the patio? what about fingers that felt
like guitar strings, tongue that tasted like poetry?
what about not being able to pinpoint exactly why;
just an unexplainable knowing? what about my spine
imprinted on the wall? what about seeing stars?
what about pupils that locked
like they'd always been destined to meet?

what about tomorrow?

IMPERMANENCE
after Alex Dimitrov

cereus bloom, their tongues—
briefly golden—night crawling
toward moonlight. sight so rare.
like catching a ghost
on midnight's film. jupiter
and saturn tied
at the waist. like us,
briefly scarlet, now ash.
blood stops. summer ends.
someday this sun who has only
ever warmed us will burn us
to a buoyed grave.
but weren't we something?
briefly bright and beautiful?

BLUE PURPLE PINK

green was seventeen.
teal were my irises
wet.

b was a dive bar
wrapped in barbed wire.
steel,
my heart after.

i n v i s i b l e, the string
tying you to me.

YOU CAN'T HAVE IT ALL
after @hungryforspirits after Barbara Ras

but you can have cake for breakfast,
wine on a tuesday, blueberry apple
cinnamon pancakes at midnight;

tintinnabulation of snowflakes
pinging against the window, a bridge that overlooks
the creek when it's halfway frozen over,
her sandy bottom squirmed between your toes in July.

you cannot take home Eindhoven or Prague,
hold Vienna concertos within your midwest walls.
but you can have a Dutch chestnut that knocks
against your desk drawer's walls
every time you reach for a sticky note or pencil.

you can have 4 a.m., whole world to yourself,
fingertips and keys typing ghosts into poetry.
delfinium dusks, tangerine dawns. you can have

what no one else has: this nook, this gallery of muses,
this stack of books and homemade vanilla lattes atop
a wooden table your partner's father built, sanded,
stained with his own bare hands.

you cannot have it all, but two years after moving in,
you can discover a plum tree in your backyard,
you can sink your teeth in, let the juice cascade
down your lips, your chin, and call it a poem.

PATAGONIA

after Kate Clanchy

I said perhaps Patagonia and pictured the sun
cracking like an egg over the lake,
a tug on a homemade line—fastened to a hook
speared through a limpet—mouth falling open
in unexplainable joy—every catch a miracle,
a triumph. This is the fairytale I need.

I wake in the cabin you erected—logs you axed
and hauled from the earth, hammered down
into the trenches you dug with an elk jaw—and I
insulated with moss. I make a morning catch—grayling
and trout—get the fire going and let you sleep off
yesterday's aches while breakfast sizzles in the cast iron.

Would you trust me not to lose the fish? To know the difference
between the orange peel kind of mushroom
that will sustain you for a week
and the kind that'll leave you gut punched and keeled over?
Would you trust me to make all
my one hundred and fifteen pounds bigger than a bear?
To not hoard the smoked meat, know
when my body is set to break?
To not tip the canoe? Leave the rosehips and the crabs
for the birds so we don't disintegrate
to bone before we've really lived?

When I spoke of Patagonia, I meant
your back against mine. I meant divide
and conquer. Suffer through every winter
just to rise like cardinal and goldfinch in spring.

I meant a thousand wooden spoons.
All of them carved with you.

WHILE LISTENING TO TAYLOR SWIFT'S "AUGUST"

it's five p.m. on a monday night and i'm running out of pages
to articulate the way taylor's haunting lyrics
bring salted winds of August to my December bedsheets.
and i'm thinking about my first love,
how i still catch our reflection in mirrors, how it feels like sun
between my thighs and an ache that starts
deep down at the etched bone, how they'll have to burn
me to ash before your ghost is really gone.
i'm thinking about the passenger seat of your truck, all that sticky leather,
all the songs i can't listen to because they remind me too much
of your palm on my thigh, hand on the back of my neck.
how it feels like another life, a mellow dream
rushing in on gossamer wind, all diaphanous, silk, and liminal.

i'm thinking of summer of '06. that in-between that twinges
like nostalgia in my chest. that mix of fever and fear when an ending
slow drips into a beginning. and i'm thinking of that night
i drank too many smirnoffs and crawled dizzy into bed
well after the clock struck, waiting for the spins to stop. and i don't
remember the gap of time between when
you lunged at me from across the couch
and coming back home, praying to the gods that mom
wouldn't wake to catch my pupils stretched to a howl.

i'm thinking of that fall, how desperately i needed to meet you
after just one glimpse from across the room, how long i saved that bouquet
because it was the first time someone had given me anything
beautiful. and i'm thinking about how my sixteen
and seventeen doomed us before we met, how you kissed me right there
in front of everyone, and i jerked back, pupils fighting
to let the light in, how that was the first of a handful of times
i would hurt you. (how a year later, it took me a month to hold
my first boyfriend's hand in public because i wasn't used to it:
wanting to be seen.) how, long after you'd given up, you'd still carry me,
stomach-pulsing drunk, lay towels down on the tile
to keep my icy bones from getting colder.

and i'm thinking of kisses at red lights, fogging up windows
in playground parking lots, how you'd (almost) always show up

when i called—except the one time i needed someone most.
and i'm thinking of all the lovers who were never mine
but how i'd play pretend for a night. how *folkore* fills me
with such tangible nostalgia, it breaks my heart and floods
my eyes with grief. how i'll listen till the record's scratched,
like walking haunted halls, like sleeping in a cemetery,
'til all the salt spills from the sea.

NOTES

"World Series Kind of Stuff" is a loosely ruled erasure poem of the song "seven" by Taylor Swift.

"Every Poet Needs a Muse (& Darling, You Were Mine)" is a loosely ruled erasure poem of the song "the lakes" by Taylor Swift.

"You Like This Poem Because" is after a poem of the same title by M.G Hughes.

The poem "You Gave Me Your Word (But That Didn't Matter)" is after a line from the song "traitor" by Olivia Rodrigo.

"Moth Bellied" is an erasure poem of the song "cardigan" by Taylor Swift.

"Kismet" is after a poem by Solomon Elijah.

"August Blackout" is an erasure poem of the song "august" by Taylor Swift.

The poem "When You Had Not Touched Me Yet" is after a line from the song "The Night We Met" by Lord Huron.

"Mad" is an erasure poem of the song "mad woman" by Taylor Swift.

"The Wake" is an erasure poem of the song "my tears ricochet" by Taylor Swift.

"If You'd Been the One" is an erasure poem of the song "the 1" by Taylor Swift.

"You Said Forever Now I Drive Alone Past Your Street" is after a poem of the same title by Natalia Vela after Olivia Rodrigo. The title is a line from the song "drivers license" by Rodrigo.

"I'm Listening to Taylor Swift's New Album" is after the poem "i'm listening to Phoebe Bridgers' new album" by Natalia Vela.

"Fucking in Memorial Park" is after the poem "Fucking in Cornwall" by Ella Frears.

The title "Wasn't I Beautiful?" is a line from the poem "Medusa" by Carol Ann Duffy.

"To the Boy Who Thinks All My Poems are About Him" is a loosely ruled erasure poem of the song "peace" by Taylor Swift.

"The Poet at Seven" is after the poem "The Poet at Fifteen" by Erika Sánchez, which is after the poem "The Poet at Seventeen" by Larry Levi.

"When Daisy Told Gatsby She Wished She'd Done Everything on Earth With Him" is after a poem by Chelsie Diane.

"Impermanence" is after a poem of the same title by Alex Dimitrov.

"Blue Purple Pink" is an erasure poem of the song "invisible string" by Taylor Swift.

"You Can't Have it All" is after poem of the same title by Kate (@hungryforspirits) after Barbara Ras.

"Patagonia" is after a poem of the same title by Kate Clanchy.

ACKNOWLEDGMENTS

To Taylor Swift. For giving us the gift of *folklore*. For inspiring me to write the poems in this book, no matter how much it hurt. (If you never bleed, right?) For teaching me to write that shit and shove it into the light, even if he reads it. Especially if he reads it.

To the following poets, whose prompts and/or poetry further inspired the poems in this collection: Abigail Rochine; Aggy (@chaosinline); Alexis P. Mitchell; Amanda Miller; Amelie (@celestialtruce); Amy Kay; Angelea Lowes; Anne Sparrow; Aparna V. (@weathered_storms.hidden_stars); Austie and Bradley Baird; @io.fff8e7; Bea Lauren Reid; Bella Townsend; Bri (@goldlacedink); Bria Kiara; Caitlin Conlon; Celeste Tsang; Chelsie Diane; Eli (@cappuccinocolcacao); Emma (@youhavegroundedme); the @eunoiaprompts team; the Falls Poetry team (@aseawords @breathwords @attemptingzen); G.C. (@washingmachinepoetry); Ginger (@ayla.poetry); Jasmine S. Higgins; Kaitlyn M. (@kaitlynwriting); Karan Chambers; Kate (@hungryforspirits); Kavya Janani U.; Kristiana Reed; Lisa (@sadcafepoetry); @livvywritespoetry; Loren Dhansew; Lotus May; L.R. Sterling; Lois (@whyylois); Luna (@lunagracewrites); Lux (@poetrybylux); Mei Yan; Melissa Sussens; M.G. Hughes; @midnight_thoughts_with_latte; Natalia Vela; Neya Krishnan; Noelle Darilek; Nyx Blue; OlwenDaisy; Paul Idiaghe; Pavithra Prabhu; the @poetconnection team; the @poets.anonymous_ team; Rachel (@sleepwalkingmuse); Rachel M. Wylie; Raistlyn (@captured.silence); Raquel Franco; Robert Dominick; Sanah Singh; Sarah Montgomery; Seraphina Soloveva; Sian Wilmot; Sky Rose; Solomon Elijah; @_soulpoems; Spencer Jewell; Trishita (@fine_lined); Tyler Walter; Vanshika (@letters.to.nostalgia); and Z. Elliot.

To those who I'm sure are missing from this list, please know how grateful I am for you and the inspiration your prompts gave me.

To my Patreon supporters: Denise Reynoso, Aaron Dragushan, Paul Idiaghe, and Niels Schoenmaker. Thank you so much for being a part of my Patreon community! Your support means the world to me and I'm so grateful to have you in my community.

To Carlos. For your guidance in formatting this book. For "Patagonia." For listening to all my poetry book ideas, including this one, usually first thing in the morning after you've just woken up and I've already had my coffee. For being the golden glimpses of sunlight (the "invisible string") between the dark branches of my poetry. I love you.

ABOUT THE AUTHOR

Kait Quinn is a legal admin by day and a prolific poet by night. Her poetry collections include *I Saw Myself Alive in a Coffin* (2021) and *A Time for Winter* (2019), and she is one of eight poets featured in the anthology *Solace: Poetry of Nature* from A.B.Baird Publishing. Her poetry has also appeared in *Honeyfire Lit*, *Blood Moon Poetry*, *Polemical Zine*, *Chestnut Review*, *VERSES*, and *New Literati*. Kait lives in Minneapolis with her partner, their regal cat Spart, and their Border Jack, Jesse Pinkman, Jr.

To learn more about Kait and her writing, visit her website at kaitquinn.com and follow her on Instagram at @kaitquinnpoetry.

Made in United States
North Haven, CT
03 August 2022

22202669R00046